THE BEST FRIEND

by

CHARLOTTE FELICITY DEL PINO

BOOKSIDE Press

BookSide Press
877-741-8091
www.booksidepress.com
orders@booksidepress.com

THIS BOOK HAS BEEN REPUBLISHED in memory of my daughter, Charlotte Felicity del Pino who was the author of this book. She passed away on April 12th 2021 suddenly.

Her book was first published by WESTBOW PRESS in the U.S. in May 2015. I have replaced the pen name of MARIA MARCHAN who was her great grandmother, with Charlotte's name. This book is beneficial to the young people and also adults.

Her second book THE BEST FRIEND 2 was published in February 2018.

DEDICATION

THIS BOOK IS DEDICATED to my best friend, Sylvester, who is the evidence of a true friend, and he brings sunshine into my life. He is a godly man who is sincerely happy when good things happen to me and supports me in trying times. I would also like to mention my young Bible students, who apply the Scripture in their lives and get good results. I would also like to thank my family.

IT WAS GOD'S INTENTION from the beginning for humans to have good relationship with each other or He would have left Adam by himself up to this day.

PREFACE

I HAVE FOUND THE BIBLE to be the source of wisdom in every aspect of human life. Since we interact with people all the time, I felt the need to search the Scripture on relationships and how they affect us. Too many times people hurt each other, and in some instances, the repercussions of these bad friendships can be overwhelming.

The inspiration to write this book came from personal Bible study on choosing friends. In the past I have made wrong choices in relationships, including marriage, but now, after a few years of making better choices, I have the right people in my life. They are genuine and sincere to me, just as I am to them.

Before I teach anything to anyone else, I apply it to myself first. I felt that if young people can make good choices with regards to the people they allow in their lives, they will save themselves from unnecessary hurt and stress.

ACKNOWLEDGEMENTS

FIRST CORINTHIANS 15:10 SAYS "By the grace of God, I am what I am…" All the credit for this book goes to Jesus Christ because of His grace or undeserved favor.

Jesus said in John 15:5 "I am the Vine and you are the branches, he who abides in Me and I in him bears much fruit; for without Me you can do nothing." By abiding in Jesus, I got the inspiration to write.

All praise, glory, and honor belong to Him.

I also thank God for giving me a Bible-believing family and relatives who instilled godly values early in my childhood. They include my maternal grandparents, my parents, and my favorite aunty, Shirley.

The values, that were ingrained in me developed over the years into a desire to study the Bible for my benefit. Then I wanted to help teach others what I was learning, that the Bible positively affects every single area of our lives, especially for children and young people.

Contents

INTRODUCTION

THE WORD OF GOD or the Bible is a spiritual book, yet it is practical. Therefore, it covers every area of human life. Since friendships are a normal part of our lives, it is obvious that they are referred to in the Bible. Friends are the people who are glad when things go well with us and they support us in difficult times. Romans 12:15 says "Rejoice with those who rejoice and weep with those who weep".

Although this is true, there needs to be caution. As we go through life we meet many people. Everyone will not become our friends; some will become acquaintances and, others will just pass through, even though they may be friendly. And there are those who will not ever become our friends.

In this book we will get the Bible's viewpoint on true friendship. In studying true friendship, it is well to learn about the wrong kind of friends. Too many people associate with the wrong people and get hurt. It is wise on our part if we can make the right decisions early in life, in order to avoid making serious mistakes. The consequences of some of these mistakes can be devastating. In some cases it may take years to recover, and in other cases they may never recover.

In order to get my point across, I have used Bible examples as well as modern- day, practical illustrations in this book.

We will consider the following:

- Difference between Friends and Acquaintances
- The Wrong Kind of Friend
- The Right Kind of Friend
- The Best Friend

CHAPTER 1

THE DIFFERENCE BETWEEN ACQUAINTANCES AND FRIENDS

AN ACQUAINTANCE IS A PERSON you know slightly. We meet people all the time, at the supermarket, the mall, the movies, church, school, places of business, our neighborhoods, etc. These people may be familiar to us because we see them regularly; we may even interact with them.

For example, the cashier at the town's café may have worked there for years and we might address each other by name. We may have some information about him, for example, he lives in our neighborhood, and he is married and has two daughters. The girls go to the same school with us. He also has two pet dogs, a white Maltese named Cotton and a black Doberman named Silky. Does that make him a friend? No. He is an acquaintance, because even though we know each other through his job and he lives two blocks down the road from us, we do not know each other personally. We do not socialize with him or his family.

What is a friend? The Oxford Dictionary defines a friend as "a person you know and like well". "Know" means "*be aware of something as a result of observing, asking or being informed; be absolutely sure of something; be familiar with; have personal experience of.*" To get to know someone means you need to spend time with him, see him in all situations, how he behaves when all is well and how he reacts when things go wrong. When things are going well it is easy to be pleasant and peaceful, but what in a crisis, the way that person handles the matter says a lot about him. Panic, outburst of anger, and blame are some of the negative behavior that is seen in adversity. If this person becomes your friend, he will lash out at you and blame you when things go wrong in their lives. On the other hand, composure in a difficult situation shows that this person is calm and will handle it better and get good results. In getting to know someone, this is a major factor to consider before becoming friends.

True friends are trustworthy. They know everything about each other (strong points and flaws) and still like each other. Meaningful friendships take time to grow as we get to know each other better and better. Also, you need to be a good friend if you want a true friend in your life.

Trustworthy means "*able to be relied on as honest or truthful*". A trustworthy person is honorable, reliable, upright, and loyal. An illustration of someone who is trustworthy: The manager of a jewelry store. The owner of the store travels often and leaves his employee, who is also a good friend, in charge. This person handles thousands of dollars on a daily basis; yet the employer knows that he is honest and loyal and will not steal his money or jewels. This employer can trust this individual. The employee on the other hand lives up to this expectation. This is a true friend.

Just as how we all have different fingerprints, so also each of us is unique. Although we may have similar tastes and interests, we have our own individual traits, unlike any other person in the world. These similarities in are what draws people to each other. From the time of conception to present time, we all have our own individual experiences which make us the people we are today. This is how our personality is formed and developed over the years. Even children born from the same parents have their own distinct personalities. Therefore, it is the same with friendship.

Time is the determining factor that makes friendships significant. Even when there are similarities among people, true friendships develop with time. It does not take a very long time to get to know someone, but it still takes some time. Knowing a person means that through interaction with each other we pay attention to details. Friendships also grow as the years go by.

An example of this is a man who got a job promotion in another town, far away from home. His family moved with him to this new neighborhood. Everything there was different - school, church, mall, lifestyle, etc. The fifteen-year-old daughter of the family, Karina, now had to adjust to a different school where she did not know anyone. At church she met another teenage girl, Anastasia, who attended the same school. They acknowledged each other and as the weeks went by they became more familiar with each other, both at church and at school. They joined the choir and did home-work together. These girls talked with each other; they discussed how they felt about certain matters, favorite songs and movies, clothes, make-up, hair-styles, and boys. Because they spent time together a bond formed and they became friends. Months and years went by, and by this time they had gotten to really know each other. By this time they knew each other's strong points and flaws, but still chose to accept the other as she was. All of us have strengths and weaknesses; therefore, love and respect are the attributes that will keep the friendship intact, regardless of the differences. This is true friendship.

CHAPTER 2

THE WRONG KIND OF FRIEND

PROVERBS 13:20 "….*The companions of fools will be destroyed.*" "Fool" means "a person who acts unwisely; a jester or clown; trick or deceives someone". The people we associate with will affect us in some way. If you will become like the person you associate with, would you like to be seen as unwise, a clown, or deceitful? No way! This is the wrong kind of friend to be around or to become.

An example of a bad friendship is found at Genesis 34. Jacob's daughter, Dinah, had become friends with some Caananite women, (idol worshippers – their standards were different from hers), and she used to go out with them. A Caananite prince saw her and raped her. Her brothers got angry and killed the men of that city. This brought shame to their father Jacob and they had to move.

First Corinthians 15:33 "Do not be deceived: Evil company corrupts good habits." People always feel that nobody can influence them, but that is a deception. This scripture shows us that bad ·friends or company will ruin the good character and morals of a person. We have an innate need to have friends and to fit in. This is fine, because God made us that way. Remember, though, that we live in a sinful world and there needs to be caution in this area. We should never be so desperate for friends that we get in with the wrong crowd. Desperation causes us to make rash and reckless decisions.

As a practical modern-day example, Marc is a twelve-year-old boy from a Bible believing home. All his life he has been surrounded with godly parents, relatives, and baby-sitters. All of these people contributed to inculcating godly values and high morals in him. He is a well-mannered and decent boy. At school there are boys who do not have the same privileges as Marc does.

One boy in particular, Kerwin, is from a dysfunctional background. His father is absent from his life. His frustrated mother has four children to take care of and works for minimum wages. She cannot instill anything into her children because she is always tired. Kerwin's character is uncouth and has bad habits; like smoking cigarettes, bullying younger children and looking at pornography. Remember, when you bring troubled people into your life, they come with their problems and these problems will affect you.

Kerwin wants Marc to be his friend, but Marc knows scriptures like 1 Corinthian 15:33 and Proverbs 13:20; both Bible verses relate to association and how they can influence a person. He knows that friendship with Kerwin is a bad association and if he becomes his friend, he could be affected negatively. Therefore, he makes the right decision and keeps away from Kerwin. If Dinah had chosen friends with similar values as hers and kept away from the Caananite women, shame and revenge could have been avoided.

Like Dinah, today we see many casualties of the wrong kind of friends. We must wisely select our friends because even though we mingle with all sorts of people on a daily basis, it does not mean they all have the same values as we do. Dishonesty; covetousness; smoking cigarettes; getting drunk; malicious gossiping; flirting; making dirty jokes; going to wild parties; pornography; committing adultery; deceitfulness; treachery; stealing; prejudice; and jealously are some of the common practices of people in general. These people are toxic, and should not be our friends. They will only cause needless heartache. Remember, everybody cannot be our friends.

People generally judge others by their faults, but overlook their own. Since there are flaws in everyone, being judgmental and critical is pointless. If we are judgmental, then we will keep away from people and become very lonely. God never meant it to be like that because when He made the first human pair He commanded them at Genesis 2:28 'Then God blessed them, and God said to them, Be fruitful and multiply; fill the earth and subdue it' To be fruitful and multiply and fill the earth means that God wanted to populate the earth, so we were never meant to be alone.

People isolate themselves because of past hurts and disappointments from others. This is the reason why when we study and meditate on the Bible so we will know how to make right decisions. Psalm 119:105 *"Your word is a lamp to my feet and a light to my path."* The Bible gives a clear direction in life.

CHAPTER 3

THE RIGHT KIND OF FRIEND

PROVERBS 18:24 – SAYS "There is a friend who sticks closer than a brother." The Bible gives two examples of true friends who stuck close to each other. One is Ruth and Naomi (in the Bible's book of Ruth). The other example is found in 1 Samuel 18:3 "Jonathan and David made a covenant, because he loved him as his own soul."

According to the Strong's Exhaustive Concordance of the Bible, the Hebrew word for soul is *nephesh* which means "a breathing creature…vitality (bodily or mental)…self." Jonathan and David loved each other in the same way as they loved themselves. This is true friendship. Proverbs 13:20 says "He who walks with wise men will be wise." According to this Scripture, if we are friends with wise people, wisdom will rub off on us too, and we will become wiser and better people. Sincerity and honesty are necessary qualities if we are to be good friends.

David was anointed as Israel's future king (1 Samuel 16:12-13). Jonathan knew this, including his father, king Saul. Since Saul was the king of Israel, then his son would have been in line to be the future king. This was interrupted because God chose David over Saul. Jonathan could have been easily jealous of David for the throne, but that did not happen. Instead he recognized that it was God's will because his father had disobeyed God and did not repent, so the kingship was taken away from him and given to David instead (1 Samuel 15:1-11; 16:1).

The account continues to show us that Saul became jealous of David because he was praised more than himself (1 Samuel 18:8-9). On many occasions King Saul tried to kill David, but because God was with him, he escaped each time (1 Samuel 18-21). Yet Jonathan supported David all the time at the risk of his father's rage (1 Samuel 20:30-31). He proved to be a true friend to David.

Like David and Jonathan we also expect our friends to be genuine toward us, so we also need to be genuine to them. Jesus said in Matthew 7:12 "Therefore, whatever you want men to do to you, do also to them…" Friendship goes both ways; it is not demanding and selfish, but kind and considerate. To find out what was the key to the friendship of these two men, especially in challenging times, we will consider their background.

The Bible does not give any information about Jonathan's childhood, but by his good character we see that he was brought up with godly values. His father, Saul, was not bad at first; he had a humble beginning. First Samuel 9:21 reads "And Saul answered and said, 'Am I not a Benjamite, of the smallest of the tribes of Israel, and my family the least of all the families of the tribe of Benjamin? Why then do you speak like this to me?' He said this just before he was anointed to be Israel's king. On another occasion when the prophet Samuel was looking for Saul to announce him as the king to the nation, he was hiding (Read 1 Samuel 10:20-22). Saul would have instilled good values into his son Jonathan. By the time David went into the palace to play the harp for King Saul, Jonathan would have been a man, so some years would have gone by since Saul was made king. This is why he was not jealous of David.

To find out what made David the person he was, let us go back to his youth. David was a shepherd. When Samuel went to his father Jesse's house to anoint one of his sons to be Israel's future king, Jesse did not even consider inviting David to the gathering (1 Samuel 16:10-13). In verse 11, Samuel asked Jesse "And Samuel said to Jesse, 'Are all the young men here?' Then he said, 'There remains yet the youngest, and there he is, keeping the sheep.' David's older brothers were trained warriors, so David's father, Jesse, thought if there had to be a king among his sons, then it would be one of them, and not his shepherd boy son who knows nothing about war.

David gained experience in trusting God when he was alone with the sheep. This is when he got to know God. Later on, when he accepted the challenge from the Philistine champion Goliath, he told Saul that on two occasions, a lion and a bear grabbed his lambs, and he killed them both to rescue the lambs. Read the account at 1 Samuel 17:34-36. Verse 36 reads "Your servant (David) has killed both lion and bear; and this uncircumcised Philistine will be like one of them, seeing he has defied the armies of the living God." This is why they were all surprised when he volunteered to confront the Goliath, who was challenging Israel to send a man to fight him (1 Samuel 17:48-51). David was now in the frontline and he became well known. Total trust in God was normal to David and God rescued him every single time.

David sets a good example for us in relationship with God. This is the key to why the friendship between David and Jonathan lasted, even in the midst of so many problems. Relationship with God is the most important association of all. Notice, when David killed the lion and the bear for attacking his sheep, nobody knew about it, not even his family, but when he killed Goliath, who was a giant and a trained warrior, he got their attention. This is what being close to God does to us. We become giant-slayers. A giant is any situation that is too big for us to handle. In the next chapter we will learn how to develop a relationship with God so we can cultivate godly attributes and become a genuine friend.

CHAPTER 4

THE BEST FRIEND

JESUS SHOWED US WHAT A best friend is. John 15:13-14 says "Greater love has no one than this, than to lay down one's life for his friends. You are My friends if you do whatever I command you." Jesus laid down His life by dying for us, to cleanse us from our sins and justify us before our heavenly Father. Romans 3:23-24 says "For all have sinned and fall short of the glory of God, being justified freely by His grace through the redemption that is in Christ Jesus." All means every single human being. Justified in the Greek is dikaioo (Strong's Exhaustive Concordance of the Bible) and it means "to render (i.e. show or regard as) just as innocent: freely justify, righteous." This opportunity to be justified freely by the blood of Jesus Christ is available to every person, but each individual has the free will to accept or reject it. God will not force Himself on anyone.

The following two Scripture verses show us that God is the one who first initiated the relationship to reconcile humans to Himself by giving Jesus to pay the price for all our sins. John 3:16 says, "God so loved the world that He gave His only begotten Son, so that whoever believes in Him, will not perish, but have everlasting life." Romans 5:8 says, "But God demonstrates His own love toward us, in that while we were still sinners, Christ died for us." Notice the phrases, "God gave

His only begotten Son" and "God demonstrates His own love toward us." These speak of action taken on God's part. He wants to be our friend, but He knows that sin is the barrier between mankind and Himself.

Second Corinthians 5:19 says "God was in Christ reconciling the world to Himself, not imputing their trespasses to them, and has committed to us the word of reconciliation." Reconcile means to "reunite, bring (back) together (again), restore friendly relations between, restore harmony between, make peace between, resolve differences between, bring to terms)." This is the reason Jesus died for our sins-to restore friendly relations between us and His heavenly Father. If we are to benefit from this act, we must believe in Jesus.

When Jesus died for us, He presented us before His Father as innocent, and God in turn sees us as righteous in Christ Jesus. "*In Christ Jesus*" means we are made righteous because of what Jesus did for us, and not by any effort on our part. Second Corinthians 5:21 says, "For He made Him who knew no sin to be sin for us, that we might become the righteousness of God in Him." There is nothing any of us could have done or will ever be able to do to get rid of sin and make ourselves righteous. Only Jesus, as perfect human, could have done it, and He was successful.

We can pray, *believing* that God will grant us our requests. First John 5:14-15 says, "Now this is the confidence that we have in Him, that if we ask anything according to His will, He hears us. And if we know that He hears us, whatever we ask, we know that we have the petitions that we have asked of Him." "Whatever we ask" always acts in harmony with God's Word (the Bible). We can pray for our families, good health, protection, favor, provision and sustenance, promotion, restoration, or help in any challenging situation. Our prayers can bring the right people into our lives, and we can be confident that God will answer. If you ask God for something that belongs to someone else, He will not answer that prayer; because that is covetousness, which is to desire what belongs to another.

Someone who did all this for us is certainly our best friend. If we want to be God's friend, then we need to act on it. This action is called belief or faith. James 3:23says, "And the Scripture was fulfilled which says, "Abraham believed God, and it was accounted to him for righteousness, and he was called the friend of God." Jesus is the best friend we can have. This friendship involves reading, meditating, and studying the Bible, especially on salvation by grace through Jesus Christ. Ephesians 2:8 reads, "For by grace you have been saved through faith, and that not of yourselves; it is the gift of God". We will be filled with the wisdom of God and discernment, which will put us in a position to make a wise selection of friends.

Even though as a child you may not have had anyone to instill godly values in you, it is not late. Take up the offer God has given to you by accepting Him into your life. May you experience all of God's blessings in every way as you read and meditate on the Scripture, in the name of Jesus. Amen.

CONCLUSION

AS YOU CAN SEE FROM what you read, friends can either bring us down or raise us up. This depends on who we allow to be close to us. Jesus is our best friend and we will become His friend by obeying the principles and instructions found in the Bible and by prayer. This is the most important relationship in our lives. From this relationship we will make good decisions with regards to the people we associate with. Friendships with the right people make our lives enjoyable.

ABOUT THE AUTHOR

CHARLOTTE FELICITY DEL PINO was introduced TO the Bible as a young child. As a teenager she started studying the Bible, which has been going on for more than thirty years. Although she has worked in administration for twenty years, in her private time she teaches a Bible study at her Sunday school. After resigning from her job, she extended her Bible studies to a public school in her neighborhood.

Charlotte especially enjoys working with children and teenagers. She believes that while children are still young, if they are taught the biblical principles of life, they will go in the right direction. She has observed that many children do not have the privilege of having anyone to inculcate godly values in their lives. Her desire is to instill a love for God and His Word into children.

She also reads books published by Christian authors, like Joyce Meyer's "*Peace*", "*Expect A Move of God....Suddenly*" and "*Do it Afraid*"; Joel Osteen's "*Your Best Life Now*", "*Become a Better You*" and "*I Declare*"; and Roy Hicks's "*Healing Your Insecurities*" and books by other writers. She did a course at the Rape Crisis Society of Trinidad and Tobago and studied child psychology at the University of the West Indies, Open Campus, Trinidad and Tobago. She does volunteer work with children and teenagers. She is also involved with an NGO who assists abused men, women and children.

REFERENCE LIST

- The Open Bible Expanded Edition, the New King James Version, 1985, Thomas Nelson, Inc.
- The Expanded Bible
- Strong's Exhaustive Concordance of the Bible with Hebrew, Chaldee, and Greek Dictionaries, MacDonald Publishing Company, McLean, Virginia 22102, U.S.A.
- Pocket Oxford English Dictionary, Tenth Edition 2005, Clays Ltd.,
- Bungay, Suffolk, Great Britain.
- www.oxforddictionaries.com

GLOSSARY

Acquaintance:

1. A person you know slightly.
2. Knowledge of someone or something.

Composure:

The state of being calm and self-controlled.

Harmony:

Agreement.

Inculcate:

Fix an idea in someone's mind by constantly repeating it.

Ingrained:

1. (Of a habit or attitude) firmly established and hard to change.
2. Deeply embedded.

Initiate:

Cause a process or action to begin.

Innate:

Inborn, natural.

Meditate:

Think carefully about.

Rash:

Acting or done without considering the possible results.

Repercussions:

The consequences of an event or action.

Treachery:

Behavior that involves betraying a person's trust in you.

BIOGRAPHY

CHARLOTTE FELICITY DEL PINO was born and bred in the beautiful twin islands of Trinidad and Tobago in July 1963. She was the first of three children. She grew up in a God-fearing family where regular religious devotions and church attendance were encouraged. Charlotte's yearning for a deeper level of spirituality and a closer relationship with God evolved into deeper involvement in church life. Her love for the bible was evident as she found great pleasure in reading, studying and sharing scripture verses with family, friends and others. This became a source of enlightenment, encouragement and support for others; particularly in times of crises.

From an early age Charlotte showed an ability to empathize and connect with, as well as, inspire others. Her devotion to children emerged during her childhood. Charlotte, being the first child and maternal grandchild, often assisted with the daily care-giving of her younger siblings and even younger family members during family gatherings. They all looked up to her. Up to this day, she often engages the elders of her family, community and workplace in deep conversation, listening and sharing; habitually lending an ear. She can be described as the thread that keeps the family connected as she frequently telephones, visits or makes use of social media to maintain regular communication.

She has had her share of challenges as well. Her father, who was an alcoholic, was unable to keep a job. This put a strain on the whole family and although by all appearances Charlotte was growing up in a nuclear family, her mother emerged the main financial, spiritual and emotional supporter of the family. Through her bible studies, Charlotte learnt and believed that God was able to deliver her father from his addiction. She shared this information with her parents and they agreed that, as a family, they should pray for him. With persistent prayer and declaring scripture in his life, for example, "I can do all things through Christ who strengthens me1", Charlotte's father eventually gave up alcohol. Owing to this breakthrough, her entire family accepted Jesus Christ as their Lord and Savior. Charlotte's father became an avid follower of Christ and meditating on the words of the Bible became part of his daily routine. He died twenty years later.

A very sad experience in Charlotte's life, was the sudden and unexpected death of her twenty-four-year-old brother, three months after he was baptized. Even though the family rallied together, this was a very difficult time for them. During this time of grief, Charlotte met a young man who appeared to be very supportive. They were married one year after. However, not long after he showed his "true colors". He no longer feigned his interest in bible studies or in living a life pleasing to God. He did not share her values. According to Charlotte, "He turned out to be a wolf in sheep's clothing." Charlotte longed to have her own children, but owing to the rocky and stressful marriage no children were born of this union. It eventually ended in divorce. In 2017 Charlotte had to deal with the death of her youngest sibling. In the midst of these difficulties, she remained faithful to God and her relationship with Him grew stronger. Charlotte is fascinated with nature, especially mountains, trees, flowers and rivers. She enjoys the peace and beauty of God's creations and looks forward to hiking or spending time in her beautiful garden. Her love for people in general, her family, youth and children is only surpassed by her love for the Word of God.

— Luscia Kanneh, Clinical Psychologist

ENDNOTE

[1]The New King James Study Bible (1988) Philippians 4:13.

CPSIA information can be obtained
at www.ICGtesting.com
Printed in the USA
LVHW091523240723
752987LV00003B/636